Daniele Pinton

D0117141

BERNINI
sculptor and architect

art courses

ATS Italia Editrice

Contents

Right:
"Self-portrait of Bernini in middle age"
Galleria Borghese, Rome

Times are all the same,
but a genius is always above his time
William Blake

The man and his genius

Seventh December 1598 was a special day in the Bernini household. The head of the family Pietro and his companion Angelica Galante, after six daughters, were about to have their first male heir. They decided to call the child after his paternal grandfather, Gian Lorenzo, and it was perhaps his birth that convinced Pietro that the moment had come officially to marry his beautiful companion. A happy moment for the Berninis, but no-one could have imagined that that date, apart from being a shining light for the family, would also mark an important moment, a real gift for the history of art. Pietro, a Tuscan by birth (born in Sesto Fiorentino in 1562), was an established artist who had recently moved to his wife's hometown of Naples to work, at the viceroy's invitation, on the largest monumental complex of the city's Vomero Hill, the Certosa di San Martino. And it was in Naples that Gian Lorenzo spent the first years of his life, the years that leave a lasting impression, absorbing its light, its music and its sounds. His temperament, like his work, revealed character and individuality; it was intense, bordering on the violent, rebellious, but also restless and sensitive. Indeed, his own contemporaries' opinions on him were contradictory: «A rare man of sublime intelligence, born by divine disposition and for the glory of Rome to bring light to the

world», was the view of his friend Cardinal Maffeo Barberini, who later became Pope with the name of Urban VIII. But for others he was a «dragon», or a «wicked and astute man». His son Domenico, who wrote a biography of his father, described him as «sour by nature, fixated in his work, ardent in his rage». And yet, if the aspects that distinguish a man's individual nature are destined to be lost over time, the work he has had the strength and talent to create remains. And so Gian Lorenzo Bernini, today as then, remains a peerless figure, the absolute arbiter of the artistic tastes of his time. What Michelangelo had represented in the preceding century, Bernini incarnated in the Rome of the 1600s.

The election of Pope Paul V (1605-1621), a member of the Borghese family, had raised Pietro Bernini's hopes as it had those of many other sculptors who followed the dynamics of the Italian courts in the hope of finding work, and especially after the downturn in large-scale commissions under the preceding pontificate of the austere Clement VIII (Ippolito Aldobrandini 1592-1605). Tired perhaps by his limited prospects and attracted by the greater vivacity of the court of Rome, Pietro decided to leave Naples, though he did not abandon the city before asking for a letter of introduction to the family of the new pontiff from an illustrious painter he had met there, Cavalier d'Arpino. Full of high hopes, he arrived in Rome accompanied by his numerous family in the winter of 1606 and, having found a house and workshop not far from the basilica of Santa Maria Maggiore, set to work. Rome was certainly smaller and less noisy than Naples, but that was a golden period for the city and extraordinary things were happening in the world of art, a true revolution with the innovations of Michelangelo Merisi da Caravaggio and Annibale Carracci. But what of sculpture? There was still a little while to wait: not long afterwards the young Gian Lorenzo would timidly enter the scene, immediately revealing all his talent even in his youthful works, and shaking up with a great blow of his chisel the well-established trade of stone carving. It is said that Cardinal Maffeo Barberini, on a visit to the Bernini family workshop, was stunned by the boy's already evident skill and turning to the father said: «Be careful signor Pietro that your son does not soon overtake you»; to which the father replied: «Your Eminence knows that this is a game where who loses gains».

Early chronology is always uncertain, but one date can be fixed: the year 1609 which marked the death of Annibale Carracci, an artist much admired by the young Bernini and recognised as his master.

Goat Amalthea (detail), Galleria Borghese, Rome
Right, Rape of Proserpina (detail),
Galleria Borghese, Rome

This Bolognese painter - who had engendered a new painting renaissance subsequently spread throughout Rome by his many pupils including Guido Reni, Domenichino and Giovanni Lanfranco - indirectly taught Bernini a love for classical statuary, the importance of studying the nude, proportion and ways to achieve it, as well as deformation of perspective with respect to viewpoint. Gian Lorenzo began his activities in the ten years between 1609 and 1619, and one of his first recognised works is a small marble group today kept in the Galleria Borghese, *The Goat Amalthea with the Infant Jupiter and a Faun*, which until not long ago was thought to be a work from the sixteenth century or even a fragment from antiquity. The uncertainty arose not just because of the classical subject matter, inspired by a passage from Virgil's *Georgics*, but because the rendition of the surfaces (more pictorial than sculptural) revealed a method very similar to that used in Hellenistic works. From these indications we may suppose that Gian Lorenzo's natural talent was not left to develop alone, and that apart from the continual advice he certainly received from his father, his artistic adolescence was spent in arduous, disciplined and constant study. Thanks to the commissions in which his father was involved, the young Bernini was able to participate in the creative enterprises of those years in Rome, and to firsthand real experience in the structure and organisation of building sites. His biographers Filippo Baldinucci and his own son Domenico highlight how for three consecutive years the young Gian Lorenzo remained «closed in the Vatican *stanze* from dawn until Ave Maria […] there drawing the rarest things, and everything that was outstanding and unusual». And if someone suggested he leave because it was time to go home, he would reply: «Leave me here, because I'm in love». This was the beginning of an uninterrupted series of masterpieces covering the entire arc of his earthly life (he died a few days short of his eighty-second birthday), during which time Bernini never left Rome save for a brief and unhappy stay in France at the court of Louis XIV, invited there by the monarch himself to design the Palais du Louvre.

Following his arrival in Rome, Pietro Bernini worked on the basilica of Santa Maria Maggiore where the recently-elected pope was having a new chapel constructed by Flaminio Ponzio. The chapel was directly opposite another built in the same basilica by Sixtus V (Felice Peretti 1585-1590) and was intended to house the pope's tomb along with the funerary monument of his predecessor Clement

VIII, both the work of the sculptor Silla da Viggiù. Various other colleagues had been called in to work alongside Viggiù, but none of them were close to the models of reference that Gian Lorenzo admired. The artist was young and curious, avid for novelty and severely critical of what he saw. He thirsted for the new, which could come in various forms, as did the painter Lodovico Cardi, known as Cigoli, a Tuscan like Gian Lorenzo's father, who was working on the same chapel and who, without renouncing his own artistic language, painted a *Mary Immaculate* on the dome, depicting the moon under the Virgin's feet with the famous marks that had recently been discovered by another Tuscan working in Pisa, Galileo Galilei. Pietro Bernini did not give of his best in the Pauline Chapel, though he did in the baptistery of the same basilica where he created a colossal marble altarpiece of the *Assumption of the Virgin*, generally recognised as his masterpiece. The work still follows old artistic paradigms with the scene divided into two levels and a sculptural technique that clearly aims to create pictorial effects, with beards and hair rendered with holes, the drapes deep and the figures in the foreground portrayed with greater relief. Both here and in the work he did in the Pauline Chapel the skilful Pietro gave full scope to all the secrets and tricks of his trade, the same ones that the young Gian Lorenzo would use in his first independent works but that would soon be surpassed by his new and individual language, destined to revolutionise the norms of sculpture in use at the time. Working there he also learned another lesson, unrelated to creating art in a strict sense but closely linked to the ability to control and dominate various projects at the same time: He came to understand that it is important to organise a group of workers (who must not operate, as happened at the time, as individuals making autonomous contributions) and that, in order to give a sense of unity to an architectural or artistic project, it is important to follow its development, melding together architecture, sculpture and painting as three parts of a single body. This intuition of Bernini's would prove his triumph.

If it is possible that Gian Lorenzo assisted his father on small sections under the soaring vaults of the basilica of Santa Maria Maggiore, the collaboration between the two is certain on a number of private commissions, although in these early works it is practically impossible to distinguish the two hands: the pair of *Hermae* formerly in Villa Borghese today at the Metropolitan Museum of New York and, in the same museum, *A Faun Teased by Children*, which

remained in the Bernini home even after the death of Gian Lorenzo; the *Four Seasons* for the Roman villa of Leone Strozzi; and the *Boy with a Dragon*, formerly part of the Barberini collections and now in the Getty Museum.

Before the series of masterpieces commissioned by Cardinal Scipione Borghese, the protector of the Bernini family, the lingering stylistic uncertainty and marked late-Mannerist imprint may be ascribed to the expressive capacities of Bernini *père*, but not long passed before Gian Lorenz's adherence to the methods taught him gave way before the powerful thrust of his own natural talent, as may be seem in subsequent works also dating from the same decade: *St. Lawrence* (circa 1614) in the Uffizi, and *St. Sebastian* (1617) in the Thyssen-Bornemisza Museum of Madrid. The young sculptor's skills, doubtless well-publicised by his father, drew the attention of some of the most important art lovers and collectors in the court of Pope Paul V, foremost among them the refined Florentine Cardinal Maffeo Barberini who first planned to entrust him with an intervention on one of the *Pietà* left unfinished by Michelangelo then, in 1617, commissioned the *St. Sebastian*. The following year he ordered four cherubs for the inner doors of the Barberini Chapel in the Roman church of Sant'Andrea Della Valle and in February 1618 Pietro Bernini, in the contract he signed with the powerful Tuscan family, was able for the first time to include the name of Gian Lorenzo, then just over nineteen. The work proceeded briskly and was completed in just five months, a year ahead of the agreed time.

But the young artist's real Maecenas in those years was another high-ranking churchman, Cardinal Scipione Caffarelli Borghese, son of Ortensia Borghese and of Francesco Caffarelli, and favourite nephew to the new pope who had personally supervised his education. A courteous and affable man of great taste, Scipione showed unreserved trust in the young Gian Lorenzo and, intuiting the twenty-year-old's genius, entrusted him with a block of monumental proportions from which emerged the group *Aeneas, Anchises, and Ascanius fleeing Troy*. If the layout and certain details of the work still show partial traces of the lessons learned from his father, something truly new is already perceptible as the hardness of the material bends before the virtuoso carving of the surfaces. It was the springboard to a success which, with highs and lows, proved unstoppable. From 1618, the year in which Bernini completed the first marble group, to 1625, Cardinal Scipione furnished his villa near

Porta Pinciana (today Galleria Borghese «an object of marvel like a wonder of the world») with the first true masterpieces of Gian Lorenzo Bernini: the *Rape of Proserpina* (1621-1622); *David* (1623-1624) and *Apollo and Daphne* (1622-1625). And with these works the artist's fame grew: «Cavalier Bernino [sic] the famous sculptor who did the statue of the Pope and of Daphne, [...]the Michelangelo of our century [...] is a man who arouses people's passions».

Alongside large-scale sculptures Bernini also worked on a different and very profitable genre: that of portrait busts, both for funerary monuments and for galleries. It was important not only to reproduce the exact features of the sitter in the marble, but also that the final result should have a closely lifelike appearance. As he wrote in a letter accompanying one of his portraits, «the white marble has to assume the likeness of a person, it has to have colour, spirit and life». This gallery of mute figures began around the year 1615 with the portrait for the church of Santa Prassede of *Bishop Santoni*, major-domo to Sixtus V, who died in 1592. In a certain sense this was the artist's first commission on public display. Still revealing his father's influence, especially in the depiction of beard and hair, Bernini does not contain his impatience with a style in which he does not feel comfortable, and if the composition is fairly ordinary some spark of novelty is expressed in his attempt to show in the marble the deep wrinkles

Funerary monument of Pope Urban VIII (detail), basilica of San Pietro

around the eyes. His first highpoint in this field was the bust of the Spanish jurist *Monsignor Pedro de Foix Montoya* (still to be seen in the refectory of the church of Santa Maria di Monserrato in Rome) which he concluded while still finishing the *Rape of Proserpina*. When the monument was complete the Spanish prelate invited cardinals and friends to admire it, one of whom exclaimed: «Why this is Montoya petrified!» At that moment Montoya himself arrived and Cardinal Maffeo Barberini, who was part of the group of visitors, touching the Spaniard, said: «This is the portrait of Monsignor Montoya», then turned to the bust: «And this is Monsignor Montoya». Apart from the many busts of Pope Urban VIII and his successors, with the portraits of *Francesco I d'Este* duke of Modena, and especially that of *Louis XIV* completed during his stay in Paris in 1665, Bernini went beyond the traditional forms of representation and, with absolutely unprecedented originality, managed to solve one limitation of the genre: the lack of arms. The solution he devised was entirely in the material itself, broad flowing drapery covered the absence of the limbs but at the same time suggested their presence.

On 5 February 1629, six days after the death of Carlo Maderno, Gian Lorenzo Bernini succeeded him in the office of chief architect of the Fabbrica di San Pietro. In August of the same year he lost his father and with him an important point of reference, but the role he had conquered for himself was one of unquestioned prestige with guaranteed social and economic benefits. Through his service to the popes he entered into a lineage that derived from the office held the preceding century by Michelangelo, thus realising the desire of Urban VIII, «who had conceived within himself a virtuous ambition, that Rome in his pontificate and by his efforts would manage to produce another Michelangelo». Bernini thus began a long period of artistic hegemony over Rome and, indirectly, over fashionable tastes in the European courts. It was the birth of a creative power but also the rise of a genius, the beginning of an association with the court of Rome which, over the remaining fifty years of his life, would see Bernini in charge of all work on the basilica of San Pietro, and grant him the possibility and the authority to redesign the face of Rome, working in the continuous service of six popes with each of whom, though in different ways, he maintained close personal ties. The history of art affords no other examples with such characteristics, of such creative continuity, for such a long time, by the work of a single artist. Yet it was above all

Bust of Costanza Bonarelli, Museo del Bargello, Florence

during the pontificate of Pope Urban VIII (Maffeo Barberini 1623-1644) that Bernini's labours reached truly titanic proportions, by the end of which he had created a gigantic mountain of masterpieces.

One indispensable factor for the successful conclusion of an artistic enterprise remained the organisation of the site, a practice he had observed since boyhood in the places his father worked, and even in this he managed to excel. Although we may reasonably suppose that he was helped by his younger brother Luigi, it was once again his own natural entrepreneurial intelligence that enabled him to remain ever present, continuously and uninterruptedly, without fearing any rivals, though he could not of course do everything himself, occupied as he was in technical assessments, courtesy visits, and private audiences with the pope. Before being named as architect of the Fabbrica in 1623, he had been appointed commissioner and inspector of the conduits of the fountains of Piazza Navona (24 August), master of the papal foundry (7 October), and supervisor of the Acqua Felice (7 October). In 1624 he "invented" the solution of the *Baldachin* to be placed as marker and protection over Peter's tomb. At the same time he was working on the statue of *Santa Bibiana*, planning the new spatial layout of the *cross-vault*, the statue of *St. Longinus* and the *funerary monument of Pope Urban VIII*, still finding time to dedicate to the temporary

decorations for the theatrical new canonisations, as well as to furnishings, hangings and much else besides. If we had to identify another record in his career we might point out that he and just a handful of other "colleagues" could command huge fees. In Rome's lively artistic world he shared this privilege with Pietro da Cortona, who frescoed the *galleria* of Palazzo Barberini in 1633, and with the solitary Borromini, Bernini's friend-enemy who died enormously wealthy. But the activity of these other protagonists of the Roman Baroque was piecemeal whereas Bernini was omnipresent; in order to maintain his unchallenged position he did not want to, or could not, say no. Clearly, over and above the mere creation of art, his workshop had to be organised like a factory, a complex machine capable of transforming ideas into money. The dynamism of the city, and the prestige he had managed to consolidate and maintain in the Roman court, provided an endless series of rich pickings: temporary decorations, allegorical representations, and sacred vestments created for specific religious and civil ceremonies; in addition to this were the incessant pontifical commissions, the continuous rivalry between members of the Curia, and the aristocracy. He never said no. The greatness of his talent was also reflected in his capacity to delegate, a practice that required responsibility, awareness, control, management skills and self-confidence. And if we consider his human qualities, no less refined and uncommon was his inclination for interaction with others as he had to deal, on the one hand, with evasive and even dangerous members of the Curia and, on the other, with an ever-increasing number of collaborators. His helpers had to be trustworthy and devoted: one irreplaceable figure was his brother Luigi, another was Giuliano Finelli who was with him from the start and sculpted the hair and the laurel leaves of the *Apollo and Daphne*, but was also a talent in his own right and, unable to accept the subordinate role, ended up breaking the friendship and the working alliance. Other devotees included Jacopo and Cosimo Fancelli. Bernini also had to rely on people to whom he could subcontract work he was unable to do himself, such as Ercole Ferrata who sculpted the *Elefantino* in Piazza della Minerva. Above them all, however, he always stood, alone, the master. His position as "friend" to the pope, especially during the Barberini pontificate, guaranteed him great liberty. One famous expression of this is to be found in a letter written by his mother Angelica to Cardinal Francesco Barberini, nephew to the pope. After the scandal of the beautiful but unfaithful Costanza, for which the pope had dispensed Gian Lorenzo from paying damages, relations between the two Bernini brothers remained tense. It was the talk not only of Rome but also beyond the borders of the kingdom. In her letter, Angelica pithily explains the truth of the matter: Her son has no respect for justice or for the authority of the cardinal, having entered the house armed with a sword to kill his younger brother, heedless of his mother's tears. He even ventured as far as Santa Maria Maggiore, seeking his sibling up and down the rectory, thus also showing disrespect for the house of God «as if he were lord of the world». But Gian Lorenzo really was lord of the world, a world of fantastic genius, and not only in sculpture and architecture but also in literature: among his many commitments he found time to write around twenty comedies (of which only one has survived complete), which would be performed at his house for a select group of friends.

Following the death of his friend Urban VIII, Gian Lorenzo worked under a pope with whom he maintained a conflictory relationship. The election of Innocent X was considered by artists, writers and intellectuals as a real calamity, especially after the fortunate period of the Barberini pontificate. Nothing good was expected of the newcomer who, as cardinal, had been known for a lack of sensibility and a character little given to art. Taking advantage of the new turn of events, Bernini's detractors and rivals lost no time in putting him in a poor light, laying undue stress on a moment of real difficulty he had faced in building the bell towers for San Pietro. Cracks had appeared in the south tower and his adversaries maintained that the structure had been designed too heavy. A commission of enquiry, though it cleared Bernini of any negligence, induced the pontiff to order the demolition of the towers at the artist's own expense, a wound to Bernini's pride that would never fully heal. It was in this context of difficult relationships, separated from the Barberini family (which in the meantime had moved to France to avoid the open hostility of the new court), and reeling from the blow of the destruction of the bell towers of San Pietro, that Bernini created the marble statue of *Truth Unveiled by Time*, which remained in the house of his heirs until 1924 when it was donated to the Galleria Borghese. This sculpture, done without a commission in 1646, remains an eloquent testimony of a muted but unequivocal rebellion expressed in the only language Bernini was sure of commanding, the language of art. Though incomplete - the figure of Time is missing,

never sculpted because, ironically, of a lack of time - its significance was soon clear to everyone: the course of time would ultimately reveal where truth and justice lay.

The pontificate of Innocent X (Giovanni Battista Pamphilj) coincided with celebrations for the Jubilee Year 1650, and the pope wanted the basilica to be even more beautiful for the occasion. To this end, in 1645 the Congregation of the *Reverenda Fabbrica* commissioned Bernini to design all the decorations, from the nave to the side chapels, from the floor to the wall hangings, even the ceiling. Between July 1646 and January 1649 huge quantities of marble arrived at San Pietro, but the project met with harsh criticism. Apart from the cost of buying such expensive material, some people felt it unacceptable that the entrance to the building should be more imposing than the shrine, in other words the area of the *Confessio* under the dome. Innocent X himself intervened to resolve the controversy, approving Bernini's project by appealing to the authority of the Fathers of the Church who, it transpired, had revealed that the Cross of Christ was made of four different kinds of wood. The Pope pointed out that the architectural structure of Christian churches,

Ecstasy of St. Theresa (detail),
Santa Maria della Vittoria, Rome

Equestrian Statue of Constantine,
atrium of the basilica of San Pietro

and of San Pietro in particular, reflected the design of the Cross and hence there was nothing scandalous if one of the arms was different from the others. In little less than a year 56 medallions portraying martyred popes, 192 cherubs and 104 doves (an allusion to the Pamphilj coat-of-arms) had all been prepared. At the same time Borromini was working on the cathedral church of Rome, San Giovanni in Laterano, which he changed completely, making it lighter and populating it with heads of jubilant seraphim almost one metre high, 220 in all each with an expression different from the others. A noble competition between the two artists for the benefit of the city of Rome.

The year following the closure of the Holy Door, 1651, with tireless creative energy Bernini inaugurated two other famous works. The first was the *Fontana dei Fiumi* in the centre of Piazza Navona, the area in which the Pamphilj family lived. Here the artist did not, as one might have expected, personally sculpt the great figures symbolising the four rivers, but limited the touch of his chisel to the great hollow travertine "cliff" and to the animals: the horse of Europe, the lion of Africa, the armadillo of the River Plate and the dragon of the Ganges. The irregular mass of rock supports an obelisk believed to be Egyptian, at the top of which is a dove with an olive branch in its beak, the emblem of Pope Innocent and an allegory

of the peace that pontiff had sought to achieve. Having produced this illusion of nature, Bernini turned to creating an optical illusion. In the St. Theresa Chapel of the church of Santa Maria della Vittoria he composed an unprecedented work that presents spectators not with a model of stone but with the impression of participating, as protagonists, in an event taking place at that very moment before their eyes.

Bernini defined himself as a water lover. It was his view that fountains always had to be given some kind of profound significance, that they should allude to noble qualities, either real or invented. Before completing the fountain in the middle of Piazza Navona he had already built others. Between 1627 and 1629, assisted by his father Pietro who at the time was chief architect of the Acqua Vergine, he created the *Barcaccia* fountain in the middle of Piazza di Spagna, a recreation of the wide barges used to transport wine barrels along the Tiber. Not only the form of the fountain but also its substance reflect the artist's genius: its sunken position was an obligatory choice in order to overcome difficult hydraulic problems, indeed the water pressure in this part of the city was extremely low and the jet did not get far above ground level. Here too Bernini gave concrete form to what he used to describe as «using the few, the bad and the poor quality to create beautiful things».

With the pontificate of Alexander VII (Fabio Chigi 1655-1667) Bernini was also able to leave a deep mark on the urban layout of Rome, as the new pope decided to implement a plan as simple as it was ambitious: to beautify, straighten and improve the roads and thoroughfares of the city. Rome was the capital of a powerful sovereign and people arriving there had to be overawed. Entering by the Porta del Popolo, the northern entrance to the city, the route followed by illustrious visitors had to be like a gallery of delights, an uninterrupted sequence of stage settings, surprises and breathtaking architecture. The appropriate moment to implement this plan came with what was believed to be the most important political event of the century: the conversion to Catholicism of Queen Christina of Sweden. The access to the city through Piazza del Popolo was remodelled for the royal entrance into the city, with the building of the "false twin" churches on either side of Via del Corso and the redesigning of the gate with the addition of an inscription which, initially addressed to Queen Christina, was then intended to remain as an eternal greeting to everyone entering the holy city: FELICI FAVSTO[QVE] INGRESSVI ANNO DOM[INI] – MDCLV (For a happy and auspicious entrance. Year of our Lord 1655). It is in this context, and as part of Pope Alexander's designs, that Bernini's works over the following years must be considered: the statues of *Habakkuk and the Angel* and the *Prophet Daniel* for the Chigi family chapel in the basilica of Santa Maria del Popolo (initially the two works were entrusted to Bernini and Algardi, working in competition, but with the latter's death they both became Bernini's); the *Elefantino* della Minerva near the Pantheon with an obelisk on its back, an image of Wisdom (also called "pulcino" or "porcino" because of its diminutive stature and rotundity, more appropriate to a pig than an elephant); and the long wing of the papal Palazzo di Montecavallo (Quirinal) known as the *manica lunga*. In the same period the artist also worked on successive projects in San Pietro: the imposing and ostentatious *colonnade*, a metaphorical Christian embrace of the world; the dramatic entrance to the Apostolic Palaces with the *Scala Regia* and the *equestrian statue of Constantine*; the *funerary monument of Alexander VII*, the last of a series of funerary monuments inside San Pietro which included those of *Pope Urban VIII* in the apse (intended to make a pair with the sixteenth-century monument to *Pope Paul III which was moved for the occasion*) and of the *Countess Matilda*; and, finally, the theatrical bronze "machine" containing the relic of the *Cathedra Petri*. As a non-papal commission, he also built the church of *Sant'Andrea al Quirinale* next to the Quirinal Palace, a real architectural jewel towards which Bernini felt, as he confided to his son, «a very special satisfaction in the depths of my heart [and] I often [return there] as a relief from my weariness». This group of works alone would be enough to ensure the lasting fame of their creator. When he finished the monument to his friend Pope Alexander VII in 1678 Bernini was almost eighty. He had just completed another monumental work for the basilica of San Pietro: the *Ciborium* in the Chapel of the Santissimo Sacramento, where the form of Bramante's famous *Tempietto* at San Pietro in Montorio (believed to be the site of St. Peter's crucifixion) was transfigured into a sumptuous and dazzlingly colourful piece of giltwork of gigantic proportions. Bernini was old and the moment had come to find time in which to cultivate his personal relationship with God, to prepare himself for a peaceful death. His uncommon genius perhaps made those entangled thoughts and spiritual

needs of the final years even more arduous. In his final works the choice of subjects, once amazing, now became moving. Tormented *Angels* along the length of Ponte Sant'Angelo welcoming and accompanying pilgrims to the holy city; intimate, vibrant, contorted portraits such as that of *Gabriele Fonseca*, the elderly Portuguese professor of medicine at the Sapienza University and personal doctor to Innocent X, whose gaze, devoid of haughtiness, remains fixed on some undefined point as he presses his hand against his breast. Or the *Blessed Ludovica Albertoni* (1674) - an ancestor of Prince Angelo Paluzzi Albertoni Altieri, adoptive nephew of Pope Clement X - in a small chapel of the church of San Francesco a Ripa, depicted in a rarefied mystical atmosphere, his last sublime illusion capturing the moment of death with immense technical perfection. And death also caught up with the elderly artist, in his palazzo next to Piazza di Spagna. It was 28 November 1680. He had expressed the wish to be buried in the basilica of Santa Maria Maggiore not far from his first house, where he had begun his career as a boy and where his father had been lain to rest. A simple floor tomb. His end was peaceful, save that in his last days his right arm, which had served him so well throughout his life, was stuck by paralysis. He said it was right that the arm, which had worked so much, should now rest and to the confessor who invited him to reflect on the actions of his life he replied that he would soon be meeting with a Lord who did not consider «the small change». Not far away was one of his workshops, the first, a place so sought after and frequented that would now be closed forever. The grand master, the great Gian Lorenzo, the magnificent director of the Baroque, was involved in his most exalted and difficult work: his own death.

Bust of Gabriele Fonseca (detail),
San Lorenzo in Lucina, Rome

Rome

Galleria Borghese

Aeneas, Anchises, and Ascanius fleeing Troy
1618/19, marble, height 220 cm

Gian Lorenzo Bernini was still only nineteen when he created this marble group, which reveals a lingering connection with certain Mannerist forms (the spiral arrangement) and for this reason has been considered by critics as the work of his father Pietro. In fact it was the first commission Cardinal Scipione Borghese, nephew of Paul V, entrusted to the young man whose talent he had recognised. The episode depicted is inspired by the famous verses of the second book of the *Aeneid* that recount Aeneas' flight from Troy, bearing on his shoulders his elderly father Anchises who is carrying the container with their ancestors' ashes and (a real virtuoso touch) the statues of the *Di Penates*. The elderly Anchises, his legs paralysed and his back curved, seems almost to vie, not only with the sculpture of antiquity which Bernini had tirelessly studied day and night for so long, but also with other portrayals of the elderly such as Caravaggio's *St. Jerome* in the Borghese collection, or the famous canvas by Domenichino from 1614 of the *Last Communion of St. Jerome*. The third figure of the group is the young Ascanius who is carrying the eternal flame from the Temple of Vesta. There are various iconographic references to be noted: to Raphael, who depicted the same scene in his *Fire in the Borgo*; to Michelangelo in his *Tondo Doni* and even more so in his *Christ* of the church of Santa Maria sopra Minerva (an example of how the young Bernini imitated the art of one who was a universal figure of reference for all sculptors); to a suggestion of the serpentine lines of the work of Giambologna. In October 1619 the group was fixed on a cylindrical base in one of the rooms of the ground floor of Scipione's villa. Putting the work on display in his residence the cardinal, the real lord of the city in that period, was metaphorically referring to the power he had achieved with a probable allusion to how his young shoulders were supporting the government of his elderly uncle the pope. The work also contains a reference to his own name, as *scipio* in Latin means a staff upon which one leans for support.

RAPE OF PROSERPINA
1621/22, marble, height 255 cm

Cardinal Scipione Borghese began making payments to Bernini for this group in June 1621, and it was transported to Villa Borghese in September of the following year. Soon afterwards, for reasons that remain unknown, the sculpture was returned to its crate and moved to the nearby Villa Ludovisi, a gift to Cardinal Ludovico Ludovisi who, with the change of pontificate and the election of Gregory XV, had taken over Scipione's role as cardinal nephew to the new pope. Having been acquired by the Italian State, the statue returned to Galleria Borghese in 1908. The subject comes from Ovid's *Metamorphoses* and is associated with the cycle of the seasons. Proserpina, daughter of Jupiter and Ceres, was noticed by Pluto, king of the underworld, who fell in love with her and abducted her as she was gathering flowers at Lake Pergusa, near Enna in Sicily. In her grief and anger her mother Ceres abandoned the fields causing a great dearth of food. Jupiter sought to find a solution through the mediation of Mercury: Proserpina would spend nine months with her mother, favouring the abundance of the harvests, while over the three winter months she would return to Pluto. The king of the underworld is shown with his regal attributes of crown and sceptre while behind him Cerberus, the monstrous three-headed dog, ensures that no-one gets in his master's way. The work contains an element that underlies all Bernini's sculpture: that of depicting not a figure but an event, captured in the passage between a "before" and an "after". Bernini seeks to freeze the moment. In this work the action is at its climax, the drama unfolding with characteristic corporeal expressivity. The rhythm of the composition comes from the movement of the heads and the limbs; the face of the young nymph is turned back over her shoulder and runs with tears, almost like diamond droplets. Pluto, on the other hand, makes great show of his powerful virility in his muscular marble strength, which contrasts with Proserpina's soft flesh which sinks before the god's powerful grip. The beard and hair have been rendered with particular skill, the deep recesses of the curls revealing abundant use of the drill. At Villa Borghese the group has been placed in the centre of a gallery so as to be free to be seen from all angles, and although the work is complete in every detail on all sides, it was intended to be seen from only from the front.

DAVID
1623/24, marble, height 170 cm

With his *David* Bernini turned to a biblical episode often depicted by artists of the Renaissance (Donatello, Verrocchio, Michelangelo). Continuing his attempts to "freeze the moment" in stone (something he had already clearly sought to do in the *Rape of Proserpina* and in the almost contemporary *Apollo and Daphne*), he chose not to portray the figure immediately after the slaying of Goliath (Renaissance Davids are relaxed, meditative, proud of the result of their actions), but at the very moment of throwing the stone that would kill the giant, at the very peak of tension of body and facial expression, in a depiction of effort that is manifest in the smallest details of the sinuous and elastic pose. Bernini's David is not a mere statue, like those of earlier artists, but an entire story synthesised into a statue. In all the sculpture of post antiquity, it is difficult to find an example comparable to this, not even among the virtuoso works of Giambologna. The face of David is believed to be a self-portrait, and in his biography of his father Bernini's son Domenico recounts how Cardinal Maffeo Barberini, before being elected pope, «would often hold up the mirror [for Bernini] with his own hands» so that the young sculptor could, in the face of *David*, depict «his own countenance with an expression marvellous in every way». The forehead is creased and the eyes fixed on the target, while the pursed lips reveal the force of the swing. Armour lies at his feet. The biblical episode, in fact, says that David initially put on the breastplate, helmet and sword of King Saul, but then discarded them because they prevented him from moving freely. Thus he remained naked. The strength, the real strength, that enabled him to defeat the giant came not from arms but from being who he was and trusting only in God. Trusting in Him it is possible for the weak to defeat the strong, the unarmed to overcome the armed, the humble to beat the proud. Also at his feet is an eagle's head carved into the lyre David played after his victory; the eagle was part of the heraldic device of the Borghese family. Begun in March 1623, the work was destined for the Roman villa of Cardinal Alessandro Peretti Montalto; however Montalto died and the commission was taken up by Cardinal Borghese who, in May of the following year, was already able to admire the statue in the first room of the ground floor of his own villa.

APOLLO AND DAPHNE
1622/25, marble, height 243 cm

Ordered by Cardinal Scipione Borghese in August 1622, work on the sculpture was interrupted during the summer of the following year in order to finish the *David* for Cardinal Alessandro Peretti Montalto, and resumed in April 1624. Following a practice that would become ever more frequent on subsequent projects, Bernini was helped by one of his best pupils, Giuliano Finelli, who carved part of the foliage, perhaps repeating a similar motif on the contemporaneous *Santa Bibiana*. The final result - completed in the autumn of 1625 - fully realised expectations and it was immediately clear that the marble was among Bernini's most emotive works, unanimously considered, even by the most hostile observers, as a masterpiece; a work to be judged with the eye and not with the tongue. The subject matter comes from Ovid's *Metamorphoses*, a widely-read text in the sixteenth century and a rich source of inspiration for artists and poets, who loved to depict the theme of transformation. Apollo, god of poetry, boasting of his unmatched skill with bow and arrow, was punished by Cupid (Eros) who struck him with a leaden dart (symbol of unrequited love), causing him to fall hopelessly in love with the beautiful nymph Daphne. She, however, had consecrated her life to Diana and to the hunt. Chased to exhaustion, the beautiful Daphne defends her virginity by calling on the goddess Gaia, the Earth, to be saved from her ardent lover: her appeal is heard and the instant the god reaches the nymph she is transformed into a laurel tree. But Apollo never stops loving her and, taking part of what remains of the woman, he places it around his head: from that moment the laurel was sacred to the god and became a symbol of the arts. The marble group brings together the two principal moments of the episode - the chase and the transformation - in a harmonious balance of forms, figures and surfaces which place it at the very heights of the history of sculpture. On the pedestal a couplet composed by Maffeo Barberini gives a Christian moral to the pagan subject mater of the group: *Quisquis amans sequitur fugitivae gaudia formae / fronde manus implet, baccas seu carpit amaras* ("Who pants for fleeting Beauty, vain pursuit! Shall barren Leaves obtain, or bitter fruit" in Tobias Smollett's translation).

TRUTH UNVEILED BY TIME
1646/52, marble, height 280 cm

This monumental work was not a commission but arose from an emotional need. It was conceived by Bernini as a personal reply - written with his most acerbic pen, the chisel - to one of the most crushing professional disappointments of his career: the order from Pope Innocent X to demolish one of the bell towers he had built on the facade of the Vatican basilica at the time of the pontiff's predecessor Urban VIII. The reasons presented by the pope, suggested to him by a faction ill-disposed towards the favourite sculptor of the now-disgraced Barberini family, accused him of having damaged the facade. The sculpture is a translation into marble of the proverb that time unveils truth in the end, and it is an expression of the artist's desire to see his professional merits recognised once again, something that actually happened without much time having to pass. Satisfied by the success of his rehabilitation, Bernini's enthusiasm to demonstrate his "innocence" diminished, and his many new commissions induced him to abandon the sculpture without completing it. Thus all that remains of the figure of Time are a number of models, while the surface of the figure of Truth is not finished.

THE GOAT AMALTHEA WITH THE INFANT JUPITER AND A FAUN
circa 1609, marble, height 45 cm

Until the year 1925 this sculpture was believed to date from the sixteenth century, and was even thought by some to be a piece of Hellenistic statuary. Still today, the reasons for which it was created remain unknown. It probably came into being as a sample model to "show the art". The scene depicted is an episode from the infancy of Jupiter but, iconographically speaking, it is not known whether it was supposed to transmit an allegorical or moral message, or if it intentionally concealed some political, religious, moral or cultural content. Jupiter, saved from the threat of his father Saturn, was raised by the Nymphs near Mount Ida with honey and the milk of the goat Amalthea. It is probable that this piece was one of the small statues of his youthful period when Gian Lorenzo, under the guidance of his father, was learning how to be a sculptor. If some of the details, such as the hair, still appear a little uncertain, others such as the rough hide of the goat, the delicate flesh of the two boys and the naturalistic depiction of the milk in the bowl, already provide a foretaste of the young artist's exceptional talent. The work reveals a tendency to seek expressive and realistic effects, indicative of a precocious inclination to engage with the problem of imitating nature and, thanks to the magnificent skill of execution, to overcome the limits imposed by the material. Some observers have sought to see in the work an allegory of the four senses: sight, with the interplay of gazes; touch, with the young Jupiter milking the goat; taste, with the faun drinking from the shell and, finally, hearing, with the sound that seems to emerge from the bleating goat and the bell she wears around her neck. It is likely that Cardinal Scipione Borghese bought, though he did not commission, this effervescent early piece of the young Gian Lorenzo.

PORTRAIT BUST OF SCIPIONE BORGHESE
1632, marble, height 78 cm

With his two busts of *Scipione Borghese* (1632) Bernini's artistic style reached its full maturity. Of the first of these portraits, two versions exist, both of them kept in Galleria Borghese. According to the accounts of biographers, confirmed by other contemporary writers, having seen the bust of his uncle Pope Paul V, Cardinal Scipione also wished to be portrayed by Bernini, something which, with the passing years, would become an ever-greater privilege for those who managed to get a positive response from the Roman master. At that time Bernini was emerging from a long period of inactivity. «Six or seven years had passed since he last touched a chisel, because of his many and varied occupations on the work of San Pietro». Unlike his illustrious predecessor Michelangelo, Bernini paid little or no attention to selecting his materials, and as he was concluding the bust of Scipione a crack in the marble appeared across the subject's forehead. In the greatest secrecy he ordered another block, this time of good quality, and without saying a word to anyone, in just twelve nights (according to his son Domenico it took only three) he completed the work from scratch, thus obtaining a second finished portrait.

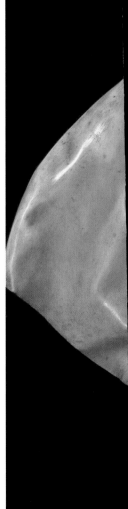

Capitoline Museums

Palazzo dei Conservatori
Sala degli Orazi e curiazi:

Monument to Urban VIII
1635, marble, height 250 cm excluding base

Despite the fact that in the year 1590 an edict had been issued prohibiting the erection on the Capitoline Hill of monuments celebrating living popes, on 13 October 1635 it was the *Conservatori* of the Palazzo themselves who decided to commission a marble statue of Pope Urban VIII (Maffeo Barberini), then reigning, to put on display in the Sala dei Capitani. The commission was given to Bernini, who was closely linked to the Barberini family and whose star was then in the ascendant. By 24 June 1640 he had completed the work and the following September, with no ceremony or public participation, he put it in place, raising it onto a high pedestal in the chosen spot. Removed in 1798 at the time of the Jacobin Republic, it was returned to its place in 1817, but not on the original pedestal which had been engraved with the names of the *Conservatori* who had promoted the initiative. The statue is actually the work of Bernini's helpers and he probably only intervened with a few of the finishing touches.

Appartamento dei Conservatori
Sala delle Oche:

Head of Medusa
fourth or fifth decade of the seventeenth century, marble, height 50 cm

Donated to the Capitoline Museums by Marquis Francesco Bichi, *Conservatore* during the first three months of the year 1731, this bust is mentioned for the first time in the inventories of Palazzo dei Conservatori in 1734 when it was identified as being in the Sala delle Oche, where it still remains today. On the front of the eighteenth-century base is an inscription which, without mentioning the name of the artist, states that it is the work of a *celeberrimus statuarius*: MEDUSAE IMAGO IN CLYPEIS/ ROMANORUM AD HOSTIUM / TERROREM OLIM INCISA/ NUNC CELEBERRIMI/ STATUARIJ GLORIA SPLENDET/ IN CAPITOLIO/ MUNUS MARCH:/ FRANCISCI BICHI CONS:/ MENSE MARTIJ/ ANNO D./ MDCCXXXI *The head of Medusa, in ancient times used to decorate the shields of the Romans that they might terrorise their enemies and today the glory of a celebrated sculptor, shines out in the Campidoglio, a gift of Marquis Francesco Bichi, Conservatore in the month of March, year of our Lord 1731.* Not universally recognised as being Bernini's own, it remains one of the sculptor's most problematic works, probably completed in the early years of the pontificate of Pope Innocent X (Giovanni Battista Pamphilj 1644-1648), when Gian Lorenzo had been banished from the pontifical court because he was considered a client of the Barberini family, and his abilities had been cast in doubt by the forced demolition of the recently-built bell tower of the basilica of San Pietro (1646). For these reasons it has been suggested that the head of Medusa has some iconographic association with the Barberini family and that, apart from the mythological significance, there is a reference to envy in the image of the serpents biting one another on the subject's head.

Church of Santa Bibiana

SANTA BIBIANA
1624/26, marble, height 191 cm

In February 1624 a group of labourers working on the main altar of an ancient building dedicated to St. Bibiana, were invested by an intense yet delightful odour and, following it to its source in the centre of the altar, discovered the body of the saint inside two large red-glass urns held together with a strip of lead. Bibiana, the first of three saints whose mortal remains were discovered and reinstated for public veneration during the Barberini pontificate, was a Roman martyr who lived in the 4th century. Having rejected the advances of the Roman governor Apronius, she was tied to a column and whipped to death with a lead-covered scourge. Her cult, which was very deeply ingrained, was perhaps linked to her name which popular etymology saw as deriving from the word for "life" and, hence, as synonymous of vitality, vivacity and spiritual support for existence. In July of the same year Urban VIII, accompanied by his nephew Cardinal Francesco, visited the site of the discovery and ordered its complete restoration, a task entrusted to Marcello Sacchetti, a personal friend of the pope. The painted decorations were commissioned from the expert Agostino Ciampelli, with whom worked a promising young man recently discovered by Sacchetti, Pietro da Cortona. And to another young artist - in other words to Bernini himself - was entrusted the architectural restoration of the structure and the creation of a marble statue for the main altar. Still working at that time on *Apollo and Daphne* together with Giuliano Finelli, Bernini shows the saint in the instant before her martyrdom resting against a column (similar to the one on which she died, which is kept in the same church), with the palm in her hand and her eyes turned upwards to where, on the ceiling of the building, is an image of God the Father. Draped in flowing robes, the customary garb of ancient Rome, the hint of classical folds at the bottom expands into the billowing and graceful Baroque swathes further up. The medicinal plants, an attribute associated with the cult of the saint (alongside the spring of pure water and the column), are not held in her hand but seem to grow spontaneously from the rock at her feet, and are very similar to the laurel branches transforming Daphne's body. Bernini's statue soon became a new model of reference for the depiction of sanctity.

Basilica of Santa Maria Sopra Minerva

MONUMENT TO SISTER MARIA RAGGI
circa 1647, gilded bronze, coloured stones,
height of medallion 90 cm

One of the most innovative and striking works of
the Bernini *oeuvre*, this monument to the memory
of Sister Maria Raggi, a Third Order Dominican
who died in odour of sanctity in 1600 and was
buried in the same basilica where the monument
is located, was requested by Lorenzo Raggi around
1647, the year he was made a cardinal. A flowing
funerary drape in black basanite is positioned over
another drape in Siena yellow with a black border.
In the middle is a portrait of the nun in a medallion
supported by angels, at the top a simple cross. The
entire work, affixed to the fifth left-hand column of
the building's Gothic architecture, really does seem
to be a piece of cloth shaken by the wind which
moves the folds but still enables the gold inscription
"embroidered" on the lower part to be read. At the
bottom right-hand corner of the "memorial" was the
coat-of-arms, now missing, of a Roman nobleman
Tommaso Raggi. Raggi's brother, Cardinal
Ottaviano, ordered the work and it is probable that
the coat-of-arms in the left-hand corner is his.

Basilica of Santa Maria della Vittoria

CORNARO CHAPEL
1647/51, Carrara marble, coloured stones, stucco, gilded bronze

As Filippo Baldinucci wrote in is biography of the artist, «Bernino [sic] himself was wont to say [...] that this was the most beautiful work to emerge from his hands». It was during the difficult years of the artist's relationship with Pope Innocent X that the chapel was commissioned by the Venetian Cardinal Federico Cornaro, patriarch of Venice in 1631, who had retired to Rome in 1644 where he lived in Palazzo Venezia. The chapel, located in the left arm of the transept of the small church of Santa Maria della Vittoria, was planned as a family chapel and intended to be dedicated to St. Teresa of Avila whose image was to be on the altarpiece. The project cost over 12000 scudi, more than the entire church of San Carlo alle Quattro Fontane by Borromini, but the result was breathtaking. Within the confines of the chapel - in a close interplay of architecture, painting and sculpture - three acts are taking place contemporaneously. The main action, on the altar, is the mystical encounter of the saint and the angel who penetrates her heart with the burning arrow of God's love. The second action takes place in the loggias to either side where, carved in white marble against a grey stucco perspective background, seven cardinals and a doge of the Cornaro family watch the central scene. The third action is that of the viewers themselves, who are drawn in to become part of the enormous three-dimensional event. In April 1647 work began on the marble fronting, following Bernini's designs, while the statues were carved between 1649 and 1650. Bernini himself created the group of the saint, the angel and the clouds, using a single block of marble. The result is one of vibrant surfaces, smooth flesh and uneven clouds, animated by the vertiginous billows of the angel's cloak. Flying stucco angels decorate the entrance to the chapel with garlands of flowers, and above is Christ's declaration to Teresa during their mystical marriage: *Nisi coelum creassem, ob te solam crearem* (If I had not already created heaven, I would create it for you alone).

Basilica of San Francesco a Ripa

BLESSED LUDOVICA ALBERTONI
1673/74, white marble, coloured marble, gilded bronze and stucco,
height 90 cm, length 210 cm

This moving and theatrical sculpture was executed during the pontificate of Pope Clement X (Emilio Altieri) when, in 1673, that pontiff's adopted nephew Prince Angelo Paluzzi Albertoni Altieri commissioned Bernini to renovate the family chapel. Dedicated to St. Anne, the chapel was located in the basilica of San Francesco a Ripa in Rome's Trastevere district, and it contained the mortal remains of an illustrious family ancestor Ludovica Albertoni (1473-1533), who was venerated as a blessed and whose cult Clement X had approved in 1671. Unlike the other famous example of St. Teresa, Blessed Ludovica is not shown at the moment of ecstasy but at that of death, not a particularly significant event in her biography and the reasons for choosing to depict it remain unknown. However her youthful countenance, certainly not that of a sixty-year-old, would seem to suggest an idealised portrayal in which, rather that depicting a historical event, the intention was to present a noble iconographic expression of saintliness. Even here, though, Bernini's genius intervenes to modify the tradition and, rather than lying beneath the altar, Blessed Ludovica is shown above, set slightly back and lying on a bed which in its turn rests on a great hanging cloth, similar to that on the monument to Alexander VII in the Vatican basilica, which joins the statue to the altar below and at the same time covers and protects the sarcophagus that actually contains the body. The statue receives light from two windows, invisible to the spectator, which illuminate the scene from either side. Above is a large altarpiece showing *St. Anne, the Virgin and the Infant Jesus* by Giovan Battista Gaulli, enclosed within a marble frame also designed by Bernini.

Basilica of San Lorenzo in Lucina

FONSECA CHAPEL:

BUST OF GABRIELE FONSECA
1668/72, marble, height 72 cm

Gabriele Fonseca, a Portuguese doctor and professor at La Sapienza University, had been personal physician to Pope Innocent X (Giovanni Battista Pamphilj). By this time, engaging the services of the Bernini workshop had become a difficult undertaking and was only achievable if one did not expect the master himself to participate. This chapel was assembled using pieces that were already in the process of being created and replicas of extant works. The altar was a scaled-down version of the one being built for Pope Alexander VII at Castelgandolfo, and the altarpiece a copy of Guido Reni's *Annunciation* in the Palazzo del Quirinale (where the angel has the same name as the patron of the chapel, Gabriel). The reference to Fonseca's profession influenced the choice of two unusual scenes from the Old Testament's Book of Kings for the paintings on the walls, which allude to the development of the use of quinine to treat malaria, a therapy Fonseca himself had supported. One canvas shows the *Prophet Elisha Purifying the Waters of the River Jericho with Salt* (by Giacinto Gimignani), the other the story of *King Ahab and the Prophet Elijah on Mount Carmel* (by Guillaume Courtois, called Borgognone). Strangely enough, and for no documented reason, the bust of the client in prayer was entirely carved by Bernini himself, one of the last portraits to be done by the sculptor who was by then an old man and little giving to such tiring exercise. The bust shows the elderly physician leaning out of a square niche to the left of the altar, in ascetic contemplation of the Virgin of the Annunciation. Other niches contain busts of his mother and his wife. Bernini's artistic register is shown in all its many variations: the different rendering of the various surfaces, the delicate chromatic effects, the realism of the wrinkles on the face and of the muted gesture of the hands - the left is pressed against his breast while the right, providing an example for all those who come to pray in the chapel, is clasping a rosary. Finally, the rougher surface that creates shadowy tones for the fur trimming of the physician's cloak provides a natural contrast to the cloth of his jacket in a perfect interplay of material and light.

Piazza Navona

FONTANA DEI FIUMI
1648/51, travertine, marble, granite, gilded bronze, height 30,17 m

Defined by some as «a miracle of the world», this fountain marking the centre of Piazza Navona in the district inhabited the Pamphilj family represented both a personal and a professional triumph in the career of Gian Lorenzo Bernini. When it was unveiled, on 12 June 1651, the enthusiasm and wonder it aroused raised to new heights the fame already achieved by the artist who thus - with this second resounding success following his decoration of the nave of the basilica of San Pietro - was able to salvage his difficult relationship with the new pope, who had been openly hostile towards the friends of the Barberini family. In April 1647 the pontiff had ordered the repositioning of an ancient obelisk unearthed near the Circus of Maxentius, and it had initially been suggested to him that he entrust the task to Borromini. According to Bernini's biographers it was Prince Nicola Ludovisi who encouraged the artist to create a model, which was then smuggled into the Apostolic Palaces and shown to the pope. When Innocent X saw it he was so enchanted that he decided he could not but entrust the new monument to Bernini. Another version of the episode states that a tender was organised and all participants were requested to prepare a clay model. Bernini, however, made his model in solid silver and gave it to Olimpia Maidalchini, the pontiff's sister-in-law, who then persuaded Innocent X to assign the commission to Bernini and not to Borromini. Whatever the case, in 1648 the great block of travertine from Tivoli was laid in its foundations, and from 1649 to 1651 the flora and fauna (originally painted) took sculpted form on the "cliff". From February 1650, four chosen sculptors began work on the four giant statues personifying the four rivers: Antonio Raggi on the *Danube*, the limbs contorted with the effort of bearing the pontifical coat-of-arms; Jacopantonio Fancelli on the *Nile*, the face covered because the source of the river was not then known; Claude Poussin on the *Ganges*, bearing a large oar identifying it as a navigable river, and Francesco Baratta on the *River Plate*, the wealth of which is portrayed by the coins spilling from a purse.

Piazza Barberini

FONTANA DELLE API
1644, travertine

As evinced by the date of completion, this fountain was built one year after the nearby Fontana del Tritone. The inscription, written by Urban VIII himself, originally indicated the twenty-second year of his reign; however, the date was corrected because the pope died eight days before completing twenty-two years since his election (a "I" was thus removed from the original "XXII"). The fountain, which collects the overflow from the Fontana del Tritone, was used as a water trough for horses until being dismantled in 1880. It was reassembled in its current position in 1917 (it was originally located on the opposite corner). Unfortunately, during the reconstruction, the original design was not followed to the letter and the shell, formerly in Lunese marble, was recreated in travertine while certain of the decorative elements were changed.

Fontana del Tritone
1642/43, travertine

Bernini designed this fountain, the Fontana del Tritone, to be positioned facing the new palazzo of his protectors, the Barberini family. The fountain should be examined in association with the nearby Fontana delle Api. It was Pope Urban VIII who ordered water be channelled to this area near the palazzo that his nephew Francesco - having bought a vineyard and a small palazzetto from the Sforza family - was busy transforming into a regal residence. Inspired by the figure created by Stefano Maderno on the Fontana dell'Aquila in the Vatican Gardens, the main figure on this fountain alludes to an episode in the first book of Ovid's *Metamorphoses* in which the Triton emerges from the waters blowing into a conch shell and announcing to the world the victory of the gods over disorder and chaos. The intention was to express the beneficial future effects of Urban VIII's own actions (he had brought water and abundance to an area previously used to cultivate vines), announcing wellbeing for the whole city and, given his exalted office, for all of Christendom.

Vatican City

Colonnade of Piazza San Pietro

Before Gian Lorenzo Bernini intervened the square was formless, cluttered with buildings and unsuited for offering a dignified welcome to those who came the venerate the tomb of the Apostle Peter and the residence of his successor. Moreover, the great open space afforded no protection from sun or rain, and each time a solemn ceremony took place it was necessary to erect a series of passageways covered with awnings along the route leading from the Apostolic Palaces to the basilica. Ever since the beginning of his pontificate, Alexander VII had felt the need to find a new, more decorous and functional solution, and between 1656 and 1667 Bernini created this original design for the area in front of the new facade of the basilica. The square is divided into two parts: an oval area contained within the two semicircles of columns, four deep and having Tuscan capitals linked by a flat entablature, and a trapezial section confined within two horizontal wings which, starting from the tips of the colonnade, diverge slightly before terminating at either end of the facade. The square is thus rendered wider and lighter while the facade - distanced from the great oval by the wings which seem shorter than they actually are - remains more balanced, almost reduced in size by this optical illusion. At the same time, the colonnade possesses an independent dynamism of its own, like a dilated circle pressing outwards against its lateral confines. The colonnades (which have three aisles, 284 Doric-order columns and eight pilasters, all in travertine from Tivoli) are linked by a simple entablature topped with 140 statues of saints, each 3.1 metres high, and six large coats-of-arms of Alexander VII. In order to avoid any disproportion that could have arisen from his decision to give a curve to the piazza, and at the same time to co-ordinate the perspective, Bernini arranged the 284 columns four-deep on radial axes. He also gradually increased their diameter so as to keep the proportions between spaces and columns unchanged, even in the outer rows. Thanks to this architectural expedient, visitors are drawn to the porphyry discs set into the paving on either side of the obelisk from which, contemplating the nearest semicircle, only the columns of the internal row are visible, as if all the others "fall into line" behind. Thus the piazza has three centres - the

obelisk and the two focal points of the semicircles - which contrast with one another in the interplay of the scenographies that revolve around each one. Explaining his own intuition, Bernini outlined the theme underlying his concept of the colonnade, describing it as the arms of the Mother Church which are open as a welcome and invitation to the entire world, even non-believers: «Since the church of St. Peter's is almost like the womb that generates other churches, it had to have a portico that shows how she maternally opens her arms to Catholics to confirm them in their beliefs, to heretics to reunite them with the Church, and to infidels to illuminate them in the true faith». He gave physical form to this metaphor in a great technical and artistic

enterprise, a dynamic theatrical spectacular which becomes evident as soon as one seeks to visually absorb the immense space. The long diameter of the ellipse measures 240 metres, 52 more than the Colosseum. Before definitively completing his design, Bernini created a total of three different wood and canvas models. The first scale model, built between March and April 1657, had only one aisle. It aroused immediate criticism and the pope demanded another, which had two aisles and was completed in the same year. Despite persistent doubts, the foundation stone was laid on 28 August 1657. Five days after the start of building work Bernini presented a third model which, personally approved by Alexander VII without consulting the Congregation, defined the portico in its current form. This final plan envisaged the use of the Doric rather than the Corinthian order, and the arrangement of the columns in four rows, with a central aisle with a barrel vaulted ceiling and two side passages with coffered ceilings for pedestrians. The creation of piazza San Pietro which took ten years to complete (1657-1667), though it led to an enormous depletion of the pontifical treasury, remains one of the most spectacular architectural achievements of the Roman Baroque. Bernini, counterbalancing his own effervescent fantasy with a classical vein he had never renounced and that is represented here by the more simple style of the ancients, managed to create an ideal epicentre for the Christian world.

Basilica of San Pietro

EQUESTRIAN STATUE OF CONSTANTINE
1654-1670, marble and stucco, height circa 380 cm
north end of the atrium of the basilica of San Pietro

At either end of the atrium are two vestibules where the horizontal arms emerging from the colonnade join the facade of the basilica. The right-hand vestibule also gives access to the Vatican Palaces. Against the back wall is the equestrian statue of Constantine, visible behind a glass door which was put in place in 1980 to replace an older one in wood. Commissioned from Gian Lorenzo Bernini by Pope Innocent X (Giovanni Battista Pamphilj) on 29 October 1654, the artist began work on the great block of Apennine marble in 1656 during the pontificate of Alexander VII, but the statue was only finally unveiled on 30 October 1670 by Clement X (Emilio Altieri) who ordered it be positioned at the beginning of the Scala Regia, and paid the artist the conspicuously large sum of 7000 scudi. The emperor on horseback is gazing up at the apparition of the Cross with an expression of wonder on his face. Behind the marble group a flowing stucco drapery in imitation damask "woven" with gold, painted by Giovanni Rinaldo and Cosimo Rustichella, emphasises the impetuous movement of the charger. The subject of lively arguments because of the unbalanced and unnatural position of the horse, and criticised for the errors in proportion, with this equestrian group Bernini expresses his pictorial concept of sculpture, distancing himself from theorists of the *bello ideale*, as represented by the work of his contemporary Algardi, and reconfirming his own stylistic and conceptual originality.

BALDACHIN
1624/35, bronze partly gilded, wood, height 29 m

In 1606, before Bernini's intervention, Paul V (Camillo Borghese) had had the altar covered with a wooden baldachin of the kind used in processions, nine metres high and borne by four angels, the work of Ambrogio Buonvicino and Camillo Mariani. It was an unassuming construction, with a provisional appearance certainly not in keeping with the grandiose nature of the basilica. Urban VIII remained keenly aware of this problem from the moment of his election in 1623 and, on 12 July of the following year, engaged Bernini to create a prestigious new ciborium, sparing no expense to ensure the work was appropriate for its place and function. The artist repaid the trust placed in him by creating the most important bronze structure in the history of Roman Baroque sculpture which, despite its originality and bulk (it is more than twenty-eight metres high), fits harmoniously into the vastness of the basilica. The baldachin does not diminish but rather increases the perceived depth of the basilica, making the apse, framed between its columns, appear even further away to visitors entering the building. It is a spectacular work, anti-classical in its formal aspects, yet in many ways linked to tradition. In order not to imitate mediaeval or Renaissance ciboria - which generally had a marble spire or cupola supported by columns - and to avoid creating a kind of temple within a temple, Bernini drew his inspiration from processional baldachins, seeking always to create an impact that was pictorial rather than architectural. The effect he sought was inspired by cloth canopies, giving the sensation of a lightweight, almost mobile and temporary structure, decisively augmented by his decision to support the *macchina* on four slim spiral columns in gilded bronze. Thus he avoided the monotonous effect that four smooth pillars of such an extraordinary height would have produced. The columns, each made up of five pieces including the capital, were cast from two models made of alder wood. The pieces were joined together by brackets screwed to the inner core to ensure their verticality and stability, and the joins between them were filled with un-gilded molten lead. The division into three sections, the lowest with corkscrew fluting and the upper two with olive and laurel branches interspersed with cherubs, lizards and bees (symbol

of the Barberini family), draws the eye up the spiral from one curve to the next favouring a dynamic and ascending vision of the whole. At the same time, the baldachin recalls ancient tradition because the form of the columns reflects that of the spiral columns of the *pergula* in the old Constantinian basilica, the same columns that were subsequently adapted to be used in the Logge delle Reliquie. The bronze columns rest on marble pedestals decorated with the coat-of-arms of Urban VIII, and end in rich composite capitals surmounted by four dados with relief decorations of faces in sunbursts (another Barberini emblem) over which extends an elaborate entablature. Above this are four enormous curving volutes which, meeting at the top with a globe surmounted by a cross, conclude the baldachin. In an earlier design, the place of the globe was taken by a statue of the Saviour Triumphant, but this plan was never put into effect for fear it would prove too heavy for the wooden frame of the canopy. Four angels bearing festoons of flowers, one on each corner, are the work of Andrea Bolgi, Giuliano Finelli and François Duquesnoy, while eight festive cherubs carry the keys and the triple crown of St. Peter, and the sword and book of St. Paul. The bronze columns were unveiled on 29 June 1627 and the completed baldachin was inaugurated on 29 June 1633, although work on the finishing touches continued until 1635. The immense undertaking drew critical comments both upon the artist and his client, above all because of the system used to get hold of the enormous amount of bronze needed. First of all the ribs were removed from the dome thus obtaining 103229 pounds, to which was added a similar amount brought in from Venice and Livorno. As this still proved insufficient, Urban VIII did not hesitate to order the removal of the bronze from the beams of the Pantheon, to which the Pasquino "talking statue" responded with a famous phrase that has passed into history, perhaps penned by an agent of the Duke of Mantua: *Quod non fecerunt Barbari, Barberini fecerunt* (What the Barbarians did not do, the Barberini did). The Pantheon, in exchange for this confiscation which supplied more metal than was needed for the baldachin, was "enriched" with two bell towers, appropriately baptised by the people «the donkey's ears of Bernini», demolished in 1883.

CATHEDRA OF ST. PETER
1656/66, bronze partly gilded, Sicilian jasper, coloured stones, wood,
glass, stucco,

Against the back wall of the apse, framed between two columns of African marble taken from the old Constantinian basilica, is the *monument of the Cathedra of St. Peter*. It is an immense bronze structure inside which is an oak-wood Cathedra decorated with ivory plaques carved with scenes representing the *Labours of Hercules*. According to ancient tradition this was this chair upon which the Apostle Peter would sit when preaching, however the archaeologist Giovan Battista De Rossi, who examined the relic during the centenary celebrations of 1867 when it was last exposed to public view on the altar of the Cappella Gregoriana, concluded that only the acacia-wood frame dates back to antiquity whereas the parts in oak (fixed to the framework with strips of iron) and the ivory plaques are part of a reconstruction of the chair in Carolingian times. This theory is borne out by the presence on the upper crossbar of a portrait of a sovereign iconographically similar to Charles the Bald. The Cathedra, replaced inside Bernini's monument on 9 July 1867, was originally kept in the monastery of San Martino which once stood on the area now occupied by the pier of Veronica. In 1636 Urban VIII ordered it be put on display in the new basilica, against the back wall of what is now the Cappella del Battesimo and flanked by two simple angels in white marble. On 6 February 1656 the Congregation of the *Reverenda Fabbrica*, by order of Alexander VII (Fabio Chigi), decreed it should be transferred from the Cappella del Battesimo to the area of the apse, and on 3 March 1657 authorised the design for the new altar presented by Gian Lorenzo Bernini. The artist drew inspiration from Baroque "machines", creating a dynamic piece of architecture not superimposed on the structure of the building but rather decorating it. The old Cattedra is enclosed within a second much larger "seat", made of gilded bronze and seven metres high. The lower part has floral decorations by Giovanni Paolo Schor while the seatback and both sides are adorned with bas-reliefs designed by Bernini. The scenes depicted are *Pasce oves meas* on the back, the *Washing of the feet* on the right, and the *Consignment of the keys*, three episodes of great importance in affirming the primacy of Peter. The throne is surrounded by bronze statues of the *Doctors of the Greek and Latin Church*. The four enormous figures, 5.35 metres high with gilded vestments and

bronze-coloured face and hands, on a pedestal of black and white marble from France and jasper from Sicily, decorated with two bronze Chigi coats-of-arms of Pope Alexander VII who promoted the work. At the front are *St. Ambrose* (left) and *St. Augustine* representing the Latin Church, at the back *St. Athanasius* (left) and *St. John Chrysostom* for the Greek Church. The bronze Cathedra, though of considerable dimensions, seems to be covered in arabesques and inlaid with gold. It is flanked by two standing angels and surmounted by two cherubs bearing the signs of papal authority: the triple crown and the keys. Above the monument, in 1655, Bernini adopted the central window of the apse as the light source and epicentre for a whirling mass of angels and cherubs who, among clouds and sunbursts, swirl around the stained glass image of the *Dove of the Holy Spirit*. A typical example of Baroque decoration, and a work in which Bernini gives full expression to all aspects of his principle of bringing together painting, sculpture and architecture in a single piece (an artistic style well-described by the historian Filippo Baldinucci with the expression *bel composto*), the monument also conveys an exalted theological concept: the Churches of East and West, united in the faith of the Catholic Church, pay homage to the Roman Cathedra. The work, completed in 1666, cost the enormous sum of 106000 scudi, of which 25000 went to the foundryman Giovanni Artusi who had to smelt around 74000 kg of bronze. Thirty-five people collaborated on the project (artists, craftsmen and labourers) who, under the direction of Bernini (and during his stay in Paris under that of his brother Luigi and Lazzaro Morelli) had to resolve various problems associated with the casting and the stability of the various pieces of the monument, all of considerable dimensions.

CROSS-VAULT

The work of completing and decorating the great *Piers* (built by Donato Bramante) that support the dome of the basilica was undertaken between January 1628 and 1639. Gian Lorenzo Bernini's commission from Urban VIII was to create a home for, and at the same time to bear witness to the presence of, the greatest relics of Christianity: the Holy Lance of the Roman centurion Longinus (statue by Gian Lorenzo Bernini); the fragments of the True Cross, discovered by the Empress Helena, mother of Constantine (statue by Andrea Bolgi); the veil marked with the Face of Christ which belonged to St. Veronica (statue by Francesco Mochi) and the head of St. Andrew (statue by François Duquesnoy). On the inner surface of the piers - which are 45 metres high and have a circumference of 71 metres - Bernini created four large niches, each ten metres high and lined with coloured marble, closed at the top by a round arch and bordered at the bottom by a balustrade with 22 pillars in *broccatello* marble and Sicilian jasper. The Carrara marble statues were positioned inside the niches. Between 4.5 and 5 metres high and all characterised by emphatic theatrical postures, they are a visual indication and celebration of the relics kept there. Above each statue is a richly-decorated balcony (identical on each of the four piers) divided into two parts: at the top, over the tympanum, are four white marble angels of whom two are holding a scroll, under them the fluted pilasters frame twin spiral columns, once part of the ciborium of the old Constantinian basilica and restored between 1634 and 1636 by Jacopo Balsimelli and Niccolò Sale. Between the spiral columns a marble bas-relief shows an angel carrying the relic concerned. Having made an initial decision in 1630 as to how the niches should be assigned, the Congregation of the *Reverenda Fabbrica*, with a decree dated 26 April 1638, decided for theological reasons that the great statues should be arranged in a different sequence.

ST. LONGINUS
1628/38, marble, height 450 cm

The statue was completed in May 1638 and positioned in the niche a month later. The sculpture we see today is the final result of a long gestation period, though even now we know only two of the twenty-two sketches Bernini kept in his workshop. The saint is shown in declamatory pose, his arms wide apart as in his right hand he holds the spear that penetrated Jesus' side. Between 1629 and 1631, with the assistance of Stefano Speranza and Guidubaldo Abbatini, Bernini worked on the clay model, which was seen by the pope on 8 February 1632. Between June 1635 and May 1638 he began sculpting the block of marble, using a special technique for finishing the surfaces which are marked with deep ridges in order to capture the light. The moment depicted is that of the conversion when the Roman centurion, having struck the blow with his lance and blinded by having looked upon Christ, opens his arms and exclaims: «Truly this man was the Son of God» (Mk. 15, 39). Bernini here draws upon imperial classical statuary, not omitting to include a breastplate and a plumed and decorated helmet, but he breaks with the spatial confines imposed by the niche choosing to represent a wide and theatrical gesture, a dynamic action well adapted to the massive dimensions of the cross-vault of the basilica. The gesture, indeed, seems to extend beyond its confined frame and give voice to an entirely Baroque reinterpretation of the statues of antiquity.

FUNERARY MONUMENT TO POPE URBAN VIII
1627/47 Carrara marble, coloured stones, partly gilded bronze, height 12.88 m

This monument is positioned in the apse of the basilica, symmetrically opposite another dedicated to Paul III (Alessandro Farnese). Both of them are framed between monolithic columns of *cipollino* marble. The tomb, ordered by Urban VIII around the year 1627, was only completed on 9 February 1647, three years after his death. The pontiff himself decided the site of his sepulchre. It is a work of great vivacity, accentuated by the soft beauty of the two female allegories symbolising *Justice* (right) and *Charity*, by the fleshily authentic cherubs and by the masterfully imposing presence of the bronze statue of the pope. The figure of *Death* is portrayed, in keeping with the tastes of the time, as a winged skeleton sitting over the casket, unequivocally proclaiming the purpose of the monument. The figure is writing the name of Urban VIII on the page of the book it is holding, while on the edges of the pages underneath the initials of other names are visible, those of the men who preceded Pope Urban on Peter's Cathedra: the G of Gregory XV (Alessandro Ludovisi) and a faded *P* for Paul V (Camillo Borghese). Urban VIII entrusted the supervision of the project to Cardinal Angelo Giori of Camerino, canon *altarista* of San Pietro in the Vatican, who personally followed the progress of the work for nearly twenty years. Hidden behind the figure of *Charity*, is an inscription bearing the cardinal's name, put in place when the work was complete: ANGELI CARDINALIS GIORII/ PROBATAE FIDEI AC SPECTATAE VIRTVTI/ SEPVLCHRALE HOC OPVS/ SIBI EXTRVENDVM MANDAVIT/ VRBANVS PP. VIII (To the proven faithfulness and tested virtue of Cardinal Angelo Giori, Pope Urban VIII entrusted the construction of this his sepulchre). Between 1628 and 1631, before the monument was put in place, Agostino Radi, Giovan Battista Soria and the young Borromini were busy creating the niche and lining it with marble. The block of black *portoro* marble for the sarcophagus was cut in May 1631, and the Carrara marble for the two allegorical figures arrived in July of the same year. By December 1628, Bernini had begun preparing the model of the great bronze statue of the pontiff, which rests on a brick core and was completed in April 1631. Beginning in the summer of 1631 the work underwent a lengthy suspension, save for Jacopo Balsimelli giving a preliminary form to the marble block of *Charity* and Giovanni Maria Fracchi doing likewise for that of *Justice,* both completed and smoothed off at the end of 1646. Activity resumed in 1639 with the smelting of the parts in bronze. The figure of *Death*, already designed in 1630, was finished at the beginning of 1644. Niccolò Sale completed the marble part of the sarcophagus at the end of 1642 and the coat-of-arms of the Barberini family in 1646. The emblem is flanked with two cherubs by Lazzaro Morelli and adorned with festoons of olives modelled by Antonio Giorgetti and cast by Giovanni Artusi.

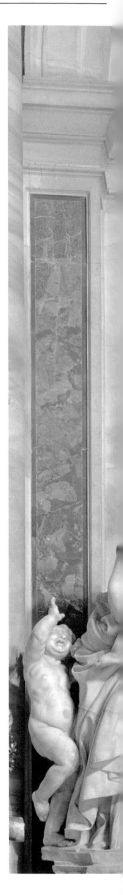

FUNERARY MONUMENT TO THE COUNTESS MATILDA CANOSSA
1633/44, marble

This piece was commissioned at the end of 1633. Urban VIII had a particular veneration for the memory of Matilda and, in the years prior to his election, had written a literary composition celebrating the famous female warrior in verse. His desire to honour her with a tomb inside the Vatican basilica culminated with the transfer of the countess' remains to Rome from the monastery of San Benedetto Po, near Mantua. In the late winter of 1644, the body was taken from Castel Sant'Angelo to the basilica where the finished monument was ready to house it. One of the most powerful women of the Middle Ages and a benefactor of the Holy See, she was to be remembered forever in the largest church of Christendom, her marble-sculpted image inaugurating a series of tombs dedicated to women in San Pietro, which continued with Queen Christina of Sweden and Queen Maria Clementina Sobieski. By order of the pope, between December 1633 and March 1634 2000 scudi were allocated for the project, to which a further 1500 were added in May 1638. Work began at great pace in the spring of 1634 and the monument entire was unveiled to the public and inaugurated on 21 March 1637, feast of St. Benedict (although the inscription bears the date of 1635). As would often happen subsequently, Bernini called on the services of a large group of helpers: Agostino Radi and Alessandro Loreti prepared the architectural structure, while Giuseppe Balsimelli and Niccolò Sale gave preliminary form to the statue, which was then sculpted by Bernini himself. Between March 1634 and February 1636 Stefano Speranza completed the bas-relief, which depicts the historic episode of Gregory VII granting forgiveness to Emperor Henry IV at Canossa on 28 January 1077, in the presence of the Countess Matilda, her son Amadeus and Abbot Hugh of Cluny. Over the sarcophagus are two cherubs with a scroll, the one on the right is by Gian Lorenzo's brother Luigi Bernini, the other by Andrea Bolgi who also carved the scroll itself and the inscription. Matteo Bonarelli, Andrea Bolgi and Lorenzo Flori sculpted the cherubs over the arch with the crown and the heraldic device with a pomegranate and the motto: TVETVR ET VNIT (Protect and Unite).

FUNERARY MONUMENT TO POPE ALEXANDER VII
1671/78 Carrara marble, Sicilian jasper, coloured stones, gilded bronze,
height circa 12 m

Located over a doorway which leads into Vatican City State, the monument
was commissioned by the pontiff himself during the early years of his reign,
but when he died on 22 May 1667 the work had yet to begin. His successor
Clement IX (Giulio Rospigliosi), who had been secretary of State, suspended
the project because he wanted Alexander's tomb and his own to be positioned
facing one another in the choir of the basilica of Santa Maria Maggiore. The
brevity of his pontificate prevented him from putting this plan into effect
and his successor Clement X (Emilio Altieri) decided to respect the wishes
of Alexander VII, although the financial burden of the work was entirely
assumed by Alexander's nephew Cardinal Flavio Chigi. Having identified the
location, in order to create the space necessary for the monument it proved
necessary to remove a fresco by Giovan Francesco Romanelli and to move
the doorway forwards. Bernini solved this latter problem by making the door
a symbolic entrance to eternity, using the theatrical expedient of a bulging
drape lifted by a skeleton holding an hourglass. To create the drape, in May
1672 Lazzaro Morelli made a clay model which he then took to the quarries
at Tivoli and, having identified the right block of travertine, had it roughly
sculpted then transported ready-made to Rome where it was subsequently
covered in Sicilian jasper. The polychrome monument, richly adorned in
precious marbles including *breccia* marble from Sette Bassi, is further enriched
by the gilded stucco of the vault which provides an effective contrast to
the marble whiteness of the allegorical figures. Gian Lorenzo Bernini did
not participate at any stage of the work although the design is his and he
supervised the sculptors as they translated his project into marble, perhaps
only intervening to put on the finishing touches in the presence of the pope.
The process of creating the monument may be divided into phases: finding
the marble and preparing the blocks; the sculpting of the figures by Bernini's
helpers: *Charity* (left) by Giuseppe Mazzuoli; *Truth* (right) begun by Lazzaro
Morelli in November 1673 and finished by Giulio Cartari in December 1675;
Prudence (the bust behind Charity) begun by Giuseppe Baratta in August
1675 and finished by Giulio Cartari in November 1677, and *Justice* (the bust
behind Truth) by Giulio Cartari, finished in 1677. The figure of the *Pope* was
done by Michel Maille who completed the ornamental parts of the vestments,
cloak and crown with the help of Giulio Cartari and Domenico Bassadonna.
The bronze sections are the work of Girolamo Lucenti and Carlo Mattei.
When the work was almost complete the new pope, Innocent XI (Benedetto
Odescalchi), voiced an objection to the nudity of the figure of *Truth* and
Bernini was obliged to cover the statue with a bronze vestment, modelled by
Filippo Carcani and cast by Girolamo Lucenti at the end of 1678.

ALTAR OF THE CHAPEL OF THE SANTISSIMO SACRAMENTO
1672/74, gilded bronze, lapis lazuli, coloured marble, height 584 cm

The epicentre of the Chapel of the Santissimo Sacramento is the *altar*, which stands out for the rarity of its marble. Restructured by Sebastiano and Bartolomeo Bianchi in 1674, it is adorned on either side with the coat-of-arms of Clement X (Emilio Altieri) who patronised the project. At the top is Gian Lorenzo Bernini's *Ciborium*, originally commissioned by Urban VIII in 1629 but only completed nearly fifty years later during the reign of Clement X. In this work - which is notable for the contrast of the gold and silver with the dark blue lapis lazuli - the artist created a harmonious piece of monumental jewellery. Inspired by architectural models of the preceding century (Donato Bramante's *Tempietto* at San Pietro in Montorio, the dome of San Pietro, and Jacopo Sansovino's altar in the basilica of Santa Croce in Gerusalemme), the work reveals its Baroque spirit in the decorations at the top, with the twelve Apostles and the Saviour on the cupola. Two large bronze angels, cast by Belardino Danese between 1673 and January 1674, represent a theme that had been very dear to Bernini since the beginning of his career. The one on the right, hands folded across the breast, turns an ecstatic expression towards the faithful, while the one on the left, absorbed in prayer, gazes sweetly up at the tabernacle. The polishing and gilding of the tabernacle, of Christ, of the Apostles and of the coats-of-arms was completed by Carlo Mattei in December 1674.

SCALA REGIA
1663/64

The Scala Regia is one of the official entrances to the Apostolic Palaces, located to the right of the basilica of San Pietro at the point where the semicircle of the colonnade meets the straight wing. Normally referred to as the *Portone di bronzo* for the great bronze door closing the entrance, the restructuring of the architecture and decorations was projected by Bernini and carried out under his supervision between 1663 al 1664 as an integral part of the colonnade. The various phases of the planning and construction were somewhat complex and no small number of formal and structural obstacles had to be overcome before the work could be completed. The entrance to the stairway proper is halfway up the long sloping corridor, marked on the right by the *equestrian statue of Constantine*, and above the archway by the figures of *Fame* bearing the coat-of-arms of Alexander VII, during whose pontificate the work was completed.

Vatican Museums

PLASTER MODELS FOR THE MONUMENT OF THE CATHEDRA OF ST.PETER
AND THE ALTAR OF CHAPEL OF THE SANTISSIMO SACRAMENTO

The Vatican collections include life-size models, made of plaster and other
fragile materials, which were used first for the presentation then for the
realisation of two monuments inside the Vatican basilica: the *monument of
the Cathedra of St. Peter* and the *Ciborium* in the Chapel of the Santissimo
Sacramento. The preparatory models for the Cathedra, kept in the Vatican
Museums, are figures of exceptional value and the high quality of the
modelling would suggest that Bernini intervened personally in their creation.
Associated with this monument are the angels (two on a larger scale and
two on a smaller) and the heads of Sts. John Chrysostom and Athanasius.
Through these fragile surviving remnants we may get some idea of the
working methods used on such complex and involved artistic enterprises.
The models of the two angels (185 cm high) on either side of the Ciborium
in the Chapel of the Santissimo Sacramento were used to cast the finished
statues. Having been employed to that end, the excellence and fineness of
the modelling led to their being preserved rather than discarded. Following
various changes of location, one is today on display in the Treasury Museum
inside the Vatican basilica, the other in the Vatican Museums. The life-size
models are made of clay and straw and the phases leading to the final form
of the two figures are well documented by numerous sketches and drawings.
The greater fluidity, the sensitivity of line and the expression of the face, as
well as the elaborate movement of the cloak, would suggest that the angel in
the Treasury Museum was by Bernini, while the other was by his workshop,
perhaps the work of his brother Paolo.

Right:
Kneeling stucco angel for the Chapel
of the Santissimo Sacramento in the
Vatican Basilica, Treasury Museum,
Vatican City.

Left:
Stucco angels for the monument
of the Cathedra of St. Peter in the
Vatican Basilica, Vatican Museums,
Vatican City.

Florence
Galleria degli Uffizi

Martyrdom of St. Lawrence
1614, marble, 66 x 108 cm

The account of Bernini's life written by his son Domenico describes how at the age of fifteen Gian Lorenzo sculpted a marble image of the saint whose name he bore, Lawrence, and how the work aroused such admiration that the Roman nobleman Leone Strozzi was willing to pay any price in order to acquire it. The formal characteristics of this piece make the story appear plausible, while at the same time revealing the debts the sculptor, still maturing as an artist, owed to the Renaissance figurative tradition. Among the various influences evident in the form of the body is an unmistakable reference to Michelangelo's figures of Christ in the Vatican *Pietà*, and his Adam on the ceiling of the Sistine Chapel. The work also provides a foretaste of other important features that would characterise Gian Lorenzo Bernini's art over subsequent years, here expressed in the skilful rendition of the flames under the gridiron where the portrayal of an immaterial element such as fire is magnificently rendered in stone, thus putting an end to painting's exclusive privilege of portraying the impalpable.

Museo del Bargello

BUST OF COSTANZA BONARELLI
circa 1636/38, marble, height 72 cm

The bust of *Costanza Bonarelli*, today kept in the Museo del Bargello of Florence, marks a real exception among Bernini's portrait works. It was an act of love. The daughter of a groom, Costanza could never have imagined she would have gone down in history thanks to the unbridled passion of an artist unable to control his attacks of jealousy. There was a rumour that the beautiful Costanza was also involved with Bernini's brother, Luigi. One morning before dawn, Gian Lorenzo ordered his carriage saying he wanted to go into the country. Instead he headed for the area of San Pietro where he had his workshop and where, right across the street, lived Costanza. He waited patiently, certain that the facts would contradict the rumours, yet it was not to be. As dawn broke Luigi, unaware of what was about to happen, emerged from the house, accompanied to the door by Costanza herself, her hair still in disarray. Blinded by jealousy, Gian Lorenzo followed his brother and, having caught up with him at the entrance to San Pietro, began beating him with an iron bar, breaking two of his ribs. Things would have gone even worse had passers-by not intervened to calm the betrayed lover's rage. However the story did not end there. Returning home Bernini called a servant and, giving him two bottles of Greek wine and a razor, ordered him: «Go on my behalf to Signora Costanza, give her these and, when you see the right moment, slash her». The servant could not but obey, limiting himself, though, to carrying out the first part of the order. The upshot was that the servant was dissmissed, Luigi departed for Bologna and Bernini was condemned to pay compensation, though later dispensed from doing so by the pope. His friend Urban VIII, like Paul V before him, was of the view that anything was permitted to painters and poets.

SIENA
Cathedral - Chigi Chapel

ST. JEROME AND ST. MARY MAGDALENE
1661/63, marble, height 195 cm

The creation of these two sculptures is associated with the figure of the Sienese Pope Alexander VII (Fabio Chigi) who in 1660 decided to build a family chapel in the Duomo of Siena. The chapel was dedicated to the Virgin and the pope ordered that the much-venerated painting of the *Madonna del Voto* be moved there. The planning phase of the chapel, then, took place between Siena and Rome, and Bernini supervised every detail beginning with the extensive use of coloured marble (the nine columns in *verde antico* come from the basilica of San Giovanni in Laterano). Of the four statues in the chapel, only two were entirely sculpted by Bernini, St. Jerome and St. Mary Magdalene. The other two, designed by him, are the work of his pupils Antonio Raggi (St. Bernardino) and Ercole Ferrata (St. Catherine of Siena). Mary Magdalene is depicted at the end of her life, when as a hermit she sought to atone for her sins. She is shown leaning, her foot resting on the bowl containing the ointment with which she anointed Christ's feet. Likewise, the portrayal of St. Jerome does not bring out the scholarly aspects of his personality, nor his dignity as cardinal, but the period he spent as a hermit, embracing a crucifix in mystical meditation. The lion at the bottom, one of finest details in all Bernini's *oeuvre*, seems to be sunk back into the niche giving the viewer an illusion of depth.

Palazzo Chigi Zondadari

BUST OF ALEXANDER VII
1657, marble, height 82 cm

This bust of Alexander VII was one of the last additions to Bernini's extensive series of portrait busts of popes, though the first and most important
of the three he did for this pontiff. Beautifully finished in every aspect, the
profile is especially noteworthy, suggesting that the bust was designed for a
specific location where it was viewed from below. The details are particularly
fine, the marble being dynamically carved to render the different features,
for example the cloth of the mozzetta with its many folds, or the wide stole
with its beautiful depiction of the family coats-of-arms alternating with the
tiara and keys of Peter. The result is an extraordinarily-effective handling of
marble to create the effects of different materials.

Paris

Musée du Louvre

BUST OF CARDINAL RICHELIEU
1641, marble, height 84 cm

It was Cardinal Giulio Mazzarino who engaged Bernini to create a portrait bust of his great protector Armand-Jean du Plessis de Richelieu (1586-1642), cardinal and prime minister of France. But what seemed like a simple request born of love for art, in fact reflected a complex and subtle interplay of diplomatic relations, as well as the assertion of a position of power. Indeed, having one's portrait done by Bernini was an ambition of the powerful throughout Europe but only the pope (in this case Urban VIII) could grant permission, as he was the only person with exclusive rights to the artist. Five years earlier, in 1636, this privilege had been accorded to King Charles I of England (a bust destroyed in 1698), and therefore the prestigious homage accorded by the papal court to the English could not now be denied to the powerful cardinal. As in the case of the bust of Charles, Bernini had to base himself on portraits. Unable to work from life and hence to uncover his subject's inner nature and transcribe it into the facial expressions, the interest of this work lies not so much in the countenance as in a part of the vestment: the mozzetta covering the cardinal's shoulders where, for the first time, the folds in the cloth suggest the movement of the arms, something until then absent from busts. The finished piece was much admired and considered one of the best the artist had yet done but, having been transported to Paris, it disappointed the cardinal who had been expecting a work of a more rhetorical and celebratory style.

LONDON

Victoria and Albert Museum

BUST OF THOMAS BAKER
after 1638, marble, height 81.6 cm including the base

Catalogued in 1680 as part of the collection of Sir Peter Lely, we know from the sources that Bernini was working on it in 1638. The subject lived in the first half of the seventeenth century and was associated with the English court. It was probably he who brought Van Dyck's triple portrait of Charles I to Rome for Bernini to model his bust "of the monarch" on. Bernini began the project himself, but during the course of the work an explicit order from the pope forbade him to continue, and the portrait was completed by his pupil Andrea Bolgi, who seems to have followed the indications of his master more on the head, characterised by its "arrogant" expression and dishevelled hair, rather than on the bust proper.

NEPTUNE AND TRITON
after 1619, marble, height 1.82 m

This life-size group showing the marine god and a Triton was commissioned
by Cardinal Alessandro Peretti for the garden of his villa, where it was positioned over an ancient fish pond. In the year 1786, for speculative reasons, the
sculpture was purchased by Joshua Reynolds and removed from Rome. After
Reynold's death the work was resold to Lord Yarborough, in whose family collection it remained until 1950. Because of its original location, the inspiration
of the work (which was long identified as being Neptune and Glaucus) suggests
a reference to Virgil's *Aeneid* (I, 32) or to Ovid's *Metamorphoses* (I, 330-342). It
was also influenced by the etchings that circulated at the time of Polidoro da
Caravaggio's *graffito* decorations of the facades of Roman buildings. The piece
was also reproduced in small replicas made of bronze or other materials.

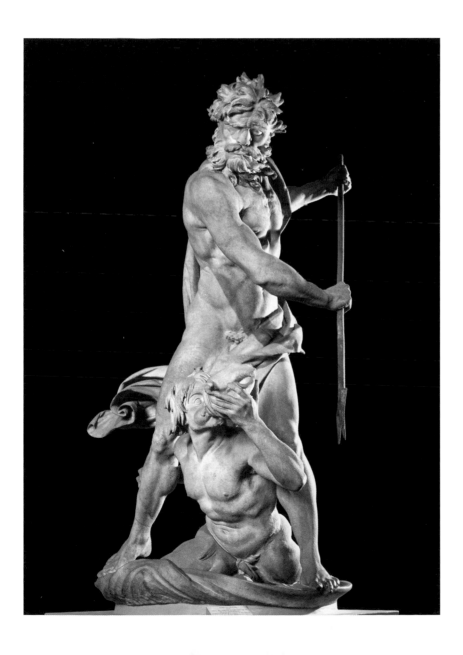

NEW YORK

Metropolitan Museum of Art

A FAUN TEASED BY CHILDREN
1614/1620, marble, height 132.1 cm

This sculpture was still in Bernini's house in 1673-1674 where it was first mentioned by a visitor, Nicodemus Tessin, who describes how he saw it on the stairway leading up to the *piano nobile*. Over subsequent centuries it reappeared on the antiques market at various times and with various owners before ending up in its present home. A satyr, no longer young, seeks to climb acrobatically up a fig tree, at the top of which is a cluster of fresh fruit. He is hindered in his attempts by two cherubs who seek to stop him reaching the bunches of figs and grapes. Although an iconographic precedent that could have inspired the subject of the composition has yet to be identified, the work would seem to represent a deliberate choice to show, in the form of an independent episode, a scene taken from the broader context of a bacchanal procession, a theme well known in Rome from various examples depicted on the front of classical sarcophagi, and pictorial representations such as the *Triumph of Bacchus and Ariadne* by Annibale Caracci, an artist much admired by the youthful Bernini, in Galleria Farnese. These were the years in which the young Gian Lorenzo was seeking to find his own path, to free himself from his father's influence, and if the layout of the composition, made to be seen in the round, still follows late sixteenth century models, the vigorous plasticity of the satyr already reveals the inventiveness and touch of the young artist.

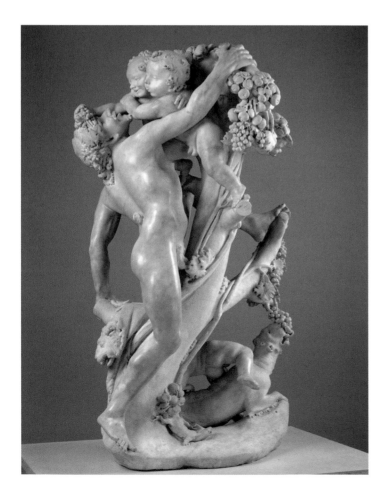

Los Angeles
Getty Museum

Boy with a Dragon
1614/1620, marble, height circa 46 cm

A youthful work by Gian Lorenzo Bernini with the help of his father Pietro. Despite the fact that he was less than twenty when he completed it, already reveals his capacities for artistic expression.

This small sculpture was made for the palazzo of Maffeo Barberini, the future Pope Urban VIII.

A hole inside the dragon's mouth lends weight to the theory advanced by some scholars that the statue was intended to be used as a fountain.

The young Hercules, who according to myth showed his divine strength from earliest infancy by killing poisonous serpents, is here portrayed as a smiling and impertinent child sitting astride a dragon's back and breaking its jaws with his bare hands.

The theme of Hercules and the serpent, frequent in Hellenistic sculpture, made a reappearance in the early years of the seventeenth century. It is probable that the sculptor drew inspiration from a classical work, but certain elements lead us to suppose the influence of contemporary events. The serpent depicted as a dragon could be a message that the Barberini client wished to transmit to another artistic patron of the time, Cardinal Scipione Borghese, whose family coat-of-arms included a dragon.

NORFOLK
Virginia, Chrysler Museum

SALVATOR MUNDI
1678/79, marble, height 93 cm

The date of this piece makes it part of the chronology of the last years of Bernini's life during which, despite the tiredness of age, he did not wish to forego the chance of sculpting (in 1678) the image of the Saviour, the sight of whom is what anyone would wish to see in the last moments of earthly existence. In 1680, nearing the end of his days, Bernini offered the bust as a gift to his friend Queen Christina of Sweden. She, however, turned it down, not having anything of like value to give in return. Unfazed, the artist bequeathed it to his royal acquaintance in his will and in 1681 the bust, considered to be his last masterpiece, is recorded as part of Christina's collection on display in the *piano nobile* of her Palazzo Riario alla Lungara. When Queen Christina died on 19 April 1689, at her express wish the bust of the Saviour became the property of Pope Innocent XI (Benedetto Odescalchi) in whose family it remained until the end of the eighteenth century when it disappeared. Various versions exist, the authenticity of which is still the subject of discussion among critics. The Saviour belongs to the group of "talking statues", which is to say that Christ's mouth is open. The profile derives from classical statuary and there is a strong reference to Michelangelo's *Christ carrying the Cross* in the Roman basilica of Santa Maria sopra Minerva.